SMALL DISASTERS SEEN IN SUNLIGHT

BARATARIA POETRY

Ava Leavell Haymon, Series Editor

SMALL DISASTERS SEEN IN SUNLIGHT

POEMS

JULIA B. LEVINE

LOUISIANA STATE UNIVERSITY PRESS

Baton Rouge

Published by Louisiana State University Press
Copyright © 2014 by Julia B. Levine
All rights reserved
Manufactured in the United States of America
LSU Press Paperback Original
First printing

Designer: Barbara Neely Bourgoyne
Typefaces: Requiem, display; Adobe Garamond Pro, text

Grateful acknowledgment is made to the editors of the following periodicals, in which the poems listed, some under different titles and/or in slightly different versions, first appeared: *poetry now,* "Ode to Fruit Flies" (December 2009); *The Southern Review:* "Poem Ending with an Unanswered Question" (Autumn 2009), "Tahoe Wetlands" (as "Wetlands") (Winter 2011); "After Visiting Your Mother, We Drive to the Rifle Range" (as "Rifle"), "I Tell My Dead Father a Secret," "Netherland" (all Autumn 2012); *Thomas Merton Seasonal:* "St. Augustine, Florida" (Summer 2009). "Tahoe City, 1988" first appeared as "Denver, 1988" in *The Healing Art of Writing,* ed. Joan Baranow, Brian Dolan, and David Watts (Berkeley: UC Press, 2011).

The author would like to thank Ava Leavell Haymon, for her extraordinary editorial care, generosity, and vision; Jeff Gundy, Dorine Jennette, and Ruth Schwartz, for their friendship and essential feedback, guidance, and support; the Art of Healing workshop and staff, as well as the Other Word's Literary Conference, for their gift of time and mentorship; Elizabeth Pollie, for her exceptional artistry and enduring friendship; her beloved family and friends, especially Mia, Hannah, Sophie, Dawn, V., Amy, Nancy, and Rachel; and of course her best friend, best husband, and basic miracle man, Steve.

This book is dedicated in memory of Gregory Humphries, artist, astronomer, aviation fanatic, athlete, adventurer, mathematical genius, master teacher, master carpenter, master friend, and all-around extraordinary member of humanity.

Library of Congress Cataloging-in-Publication Data
Levine, Julia B.
    [Poems. Selections]
    Small Disasters Seen in Sunlight : Poems / Julia B. Levine.
        pages cm — (Barataria Poetry Series)
    "LSU Press Paperback Original."
    Includes bibliographical references.
    ISBN 978-0-8071-5453-3 (paper : alk. paper) — ISBN 978-0-8071-5454-0 (pdf) —
ISBN 978-0-8071-5455-7 (epub) — ISBN 978-0-8071-5456-4 (mobi)
    I. Title.
    PS3562.E89765S63 2014
    811'.54—dc23

                                    2013022861

The paper in this book meets the guidelines for permanence and durability of the Committee on Production Guidelines for Book Longevity of the Council on Library Resources. ∞

In memory of Gregory Humphries, 1958–2012

. . . We must have
the stubbornness to accept our gladness in the ruthless
furnace of this world. To make injustice the only
measure of our attention is to praise the Devil.
If the locomotive of the Lord runs us down,
we should give thanks that the end had magnitude.
We must admit there will be music despite everything . . .

—JACK GILBERT
"A Brief for the Defense," from *Refusing Heaven* (2005)

CONTENTS

IV risking delight

V music despite everything

SMALL DISASTERS SEEN IN SUNLIGHT

At the Hog Island Oyster Company

In this summer of vast foreclosures
      crumbling into condoms and empty cans,
clouds of blackbirds drop from sky
      like punctuation marks estranged from meaning.
These days tragedies are only markings in a score
      that crescendos behind the cannery,
where someone abandoned their Kenmore
      to two nine-year-old girls hiding inside it.
Still, the world has ended before and will again.
      In the bombed-out moment
before the wrong decision, think of clarity
      as a torch for the exceedingly lost.
Think of paddling across Tomales Bay
      toward the lawless vigor of a knife
set against oysters, no doubt aching like organs,
      and your mouth, that throne of epistolary grammar,
taken to grinding through a global story.
      In the long forgetting that we call a life,
think of bivalves as a portal to sensorial faith.
      Listen, how else but through the body's doors—
the sweet flesh juiced and spiced,
      existence doubled and unhinged—
might aliveness still be tasted whole?

I

ruthless furnace

St. Augustine, Florida

A predatory lushness hums just out of sight—alligators, egrets,
a jaguar maybe, lunching on orchids and sunlight—

while the engine of amusement turns,

and a boy, dark as the coke I'm drinking, and too young to be alone,
grips a metal pony, sandals dangling above the stirrups.

In his *Confessions*, Saint Augustine wrote that the soul is a house
too small for God to enter, though it can be enlarged, remade.

Can spill over, like the foster mother in my office last week,
confiding, *It's too late to talk me out of it—*
just tell me what I'm getting into.

And the baby herself, wild with whatever swells
once it is unstrapped from torment, frantically mouthing blocks,
plastic keys, a bottle held to her perfect lips.

Who knows how goodness persists. Or why,

when I said her given name, the baby grinned up at me,
her foster mother telling me they found her in a motel room,
thighs bruised black as eggplant, her tiny openings torn apart.

Even Augustine knew that the soulless suffer no pain.

It's so much to carry, I said to that good woman.
The hand-shaped bruise where someone held that baby down.
The sheets and dirty tissues mounded over the satchel

of her slowing breath. *Still, you must remember everything*
and slowly give it back to her. Even here, even now,

beside this sun-drenched bay,
under canopies dreadlocked with Spanish moss,

do you see how that boy cranes backward to find me?

How desperately the slender narrative of a soul
needs someone, anyone, to stand at one spot
and watch what comes around.

A Week of Storms

This morning, rain softens the bones of trees
the way faith might make impermanence
bearable, if you believed.

Here, the creek goes underground.
Here, wood-ducks spread their wings and fly,

while a young woman in braids
walks the arboretum trails,
her arms crossed around a notebook,
her eyes a shocking blue.

Anything would help, she explains.
Opens her binder to an x-ray

and bows shyly when I lay a few bills
over the unmistakable cloud of a tumor drifting there.

My daughter's blind now, the woman says,
but if we hold her between us
she still wants to ride her bicycle
up and down the drive.

And then a pause
while the Pacific gathers into the next storm.

At the café, sparrows warm themselves on tables.

A day so golden and raw, it spills through
the dogs we pass everywhere
leaping, straining at the throat of light.

Either we must start over

or die like this—gilded, naked,
hearts wetted long enough to split apart
the world's difficult skin.

A homeless couple lays their sleeping bags out to dry.

The tallest trees are still raining
onto the green calderas of the lawns.

At the stoplight, the signal chirps
and five people start across the raindark street,
their white canes like a chorus of fingers

touching against concrete, curbstones,
the ceaseless fissures we walk between.

Heat Wave on the Children's Unit

Draw the best person you can, the instructions go,

and this afternoon in my office, the boy squints up at me
to see what a real person looks like.

The air conditioner rattles my windows.

Outside every breeze has been beaten into stillness,
sun merciless as a scalding brand laid against flesh,

or the searing tear of a stranger forcing himself inside this boy.

Now his buzzcut brushes my hand, a surprising softness
to the bristles,

as he sketches what isn't here: a nasty gash on my forehead,
a broken bone cracked through my arm.

Because some children are a warning for anyone who might listen,

the way a bird will sing at the edge of a storm,
or a horse might batter a barn just before an earthquake.

Because he wants to know if I can help with a bad dream,
the one he has every night now,

his house on fire, his body trapped on the third floor, enflamed

and falling.
Because this heat is the fire of the actual,

and always another life burns behind this one.

Instead of Orchids or an Elegy of Swans

gliding across a spring-fed pond, there was Danny Romeo
(*Danny by day, the women like to call me Romeo at night*),
in a pressed white shirt and tie, offering to wash my windshield
at the Arco, and then his offhand suggestion to fix two divets
I couldn't see, but felt, his hand leading my thumb
over the dimpled chips, my insurance company already dialed up
on a cellphone, and his guy in a t-shirt and jeans, strolling over
from nowhere to plug the holes Danny said would *explode*
the first cold morning, shattering your entire glass.
Clearly a scam, I should have turned away.
But when his guy injected epoxy and dried it with a blue flame,
I was disarmed by how Danny had delivered what was promised.
We shook hands. Smiled. Then, all the way across the delta,
the late summer sun blindingly gold and generous,
cattle egrets unfolding over the slate grey bay,
it seemed August was not the month
to go round the heart's four rooms
without opening the blinds, letting the wind in—
Danny Romeo, no doubt closing a few more deals
before ending with a girl in his bed,
his hands touching her carefully as if she was the world itself,
one made as much of sweetness as of damage,
or at least perched at the very beginning of disaster,
with time enough for just the right repair.

Strolling in Late April

With its complete lack of morals,
spring has tongued bud and stamen,
uncoiled tulips, seduced entire fields
into swollen cups of color.
Each time I tell your mother that you are her son,
she opens her mouth, fumbles at her buttoned collar,
raises her eyes in surprise.
How could she have made a man?
Her clipped hair is moist around her forehead.
I cuff her sleeves, kneel to roll up her pants.
Around us, light floats like a bridal cotton,
a delicate curtain drifting between worlds.
Everywhere there are maples and oaks
just leafing out, families on blankets
with ice and cakes and chips,
babies wobbling on their overpadded bottoms.
Sometimes your mother forgets to walk
and stops dead in the middle of the path.
Dogwood blossoms hover on their invisible limbs.
The Kwanzan cherry blushes, tumbles down.
Perhaps dying is just another way to live
briefly, in a world gone strange
and wondrously new.
Up ahead, a monarch dips in and out of shade.
Butterfly? she repeats after me,
eyes wide in awe.
Is that really a word?

On the Dementia Floor

Wheelchairs huddle around the television
or sit angled to afford a better view

of the finches and their handfuls of flight
inside a glass cupboard,

though the residents only sleep, fully clothed.
The translucent whites of their necks. Their hands

slipped from laps. Falling
like snow through the windows—

not just its ribbon and flake haunting the cedars,
undressing the indifferent poplars—

but how each petal seems a tiny raft
lashed to the ceaseless edge.

Oh piano, gladioli, raspberries in the basement freezer.

Oh door in water and floating past—

After Visiting Your Mother, We Drive to the Rifle Range

Oiled and easily cocked, this gun is loved.
The shells gold as a bright forgetting,
the forest silent with snow.
Who is out there? your mother had asked,
pointing to an orderly.
I hold the rifle up to my shoulder.
Squint through the sightline.
Same shoulder where your mother
laid her head and sobbed. *Sad sad,*
she said, then listed forward and slept.
Dismantle me, the body says. Or the mind.
The trees undressed of leaves
like a kind of stone against stone.
The being of us, hitched one to another,
before the discharge, the dark bits
sparked and afflicted. In the white fields,
someone had lined up clay pots
against the fresh nothing of beauty.
We would take turns. Going
first one, then another.

Small Disasters Seen in Sunlight

The swarm came from deep inside the blossoms,
bees like children laughing and laughing,

and the sound of apprehension
opening a white canopy under the tree,

all flowering deeded to a slow drift down.
It was not just the last ripe oranges I held,

wanting to bring something of this shimmer
to his hospital bed, but also the stopped film

from the camera mounted on his helmet.
There he went on jumping from a plane

into vastness, his mouth bruised
with the joyous rush of deceleration, articulations

of wind and cable tearing silence. Listen,
no matter what you believe about the soul

and its flesh, attachment has its own gravity,
the ground forever rising up too hard and fast.

In that last frame before the image blackens,
I see the shadow of his two unshattered legs,

his paired, not-yet-exploded feet,
the worship in the way he reaches toward earth,

toward us—we who know nothing of wholeness
before it is broken.

One spring. One summer.
Five failed surgeries. Twenty-nine titanium screws.

Countless Percocet and Norco.
Five months plus nineteen days of pain.

Two skin grafts. A Fibonacci sequence
of phone calls to insurance agents.

One steel rod. Four metal straps.
Twelve days without leaving his bed.

Six days of refusing to open the curtains
to the sky's last residue of light

before dusk crushes it to stone.
No warning that endurance

might be the only border between worlds.
Or that a man could heave his destroyed legs

onto a barricade—
could sling himself like a bell rope

over the roof
to let something outside the body

ring.

If circumstance was a clinic of the nonpareil
where the white of night-blooming jasmine and nicotiana
were bandages laid underneath his skin
and the nerves slept finally, dreamlessly into place—

if a day came that he woke, stepping gingerly
into the unfinished hallways that opened out to sea,
waves curled and breaking with their granted power,
that grin loping across his lips again—

then in the face of brevity,
in the beauty of how we must hurry,
could someone please torch the suicide note
taped to his walker on top of the tallest building in town?

Could they turn back the ambulance and its whining lights
driving I-80 too slow? And the railroad tracks
he landed beside, could they touch somewhere
on the horizon, instead of where his name

kickbacked like a gun's concussion,
knocking me to the clinic's polished floor?
The dead are born viciously through the living.
And memory, poor lifejacket, drowned

in the most afflicted moments. In one small window,
it was still summer, though suddenly night, the sky swept black.
I woke strangely barefoot inside the grieving room
with its box of coarse tissues and bilingual pamphlets

that warned against the stupid questions
the stupid heart would ask and ask.
I had to gather up my purse, my keys, my sandals
someone had paired outside the door.

Marked in dirt and grime, exact imprints of my weight
pressed against earth. Now past him,
the sound of one foot following another,
the right leading if. The left following then.

Dusk, and I had just left the hospital
　　and the body that no longer contained him,

　　　　when the myriad, black missionaries of sky

　　circled over the warehouse I'd parked beside
—a dark cloud shattering to obsidian snow

　　　　under a sky that flamed and burned,

　　a bluegrey washing over the horizon,
the pooling murmuration poured into shadows

　　　　brushing over concrete walls, the roof,

　　and it sounded like water
inside the larger music of their countless, weightless

　　　　turnings—so many starlings with night

　　inside and between their wings,
each finely tuned to the velocity of the whole

　　　　swarm swept apart, braiding back to one—

　　as if being was simply made
to be lost and made again, and I wept of course,

　　　　for the perfect synchrony of the flock

　　and its small, forgotten parts,
though I could see each bird had never been

only itself, never closer than now

to the dark astonishment
tucked inside the world he had just been

broken through.

Tonight I picture grief as a commuter
stepping onto the train that rides these tracks,

her small bag packed with power lines
and the dark birds that stiffen there.

Then he takes the window seat beside her,
both of them staring past the winter fields

at last spring
where a county official shot a half dozen coyotes

and left them bundled
along the highway's shoulder. Further on,

he points out the afternoon
he and I dug a poor grave, the coyotes' blonde fur

sparking under a blanket of flies and wind.
Always the brightness of it, the March sun,

he muses, and I'm almost certain
that was the same day he told me all light

had narrowly escaped matter's dark pull.
We were pouring water bottles

over each other's hands
to wash away the dirt and stink.

A bay gelding walked slowly toward us,
then lifted his enormous muzzle

over the farmer's electric fence.
I tried to imagine that kind of unlikely grace,

but couldn't. *Think,* he said,
of the mathematical possibility of a parallel galaxy,

and then multiply it exponentially
until you arrive back here,

a woman exactly like you standing before a brown horse,
willing to risk a little shock, a little hurt,

just to reach across this halved enormity
and touch.

II

locomotive of the Lord

Netherland

Imagine snow as a celestial orchard in bloom,

mile after mile of pine and granite
clothed in an empire of silence.

There, we burn newspapers, a cord of wood, a bed frame
the squatters before us have left.

Mornings, our boots make tracks
beside the split moons of deer, the clawed prints of bear,

even as wind whittles it all away.
Some afternoons, there is sunlight through the windows

and we lie inside our zipped-together bags
moving like a legless shadow.

Nights, we hear wolves with the sky inside their throats.
No one but your friend knows where we are,

and he has driven us into the Rockies at dark,
saying, "The nearest town is Netherland."

Meaning, you can't rescue astonishment
from a boy and girl lost inside the molten light of desire.

Imagine your first love as a road of crumbs
marking a path back to the awakened whole

and your future
as all the small, invisible hungers of this world

devouring the trail.

Post-Surgery Narratives in Triptych

CONJOINED

I woke, legs splayed, my head turbaned and separate, while a tiny room in my chest remembered her blink and breath. Remembered a door ajar to hunger as it slipped between us, and later, a strike of lightning as the doctors broke and broke the cage around my heart to start it up again. *Our heart,* she'd insist, her thoughts entering mine like rain just before it arrives. *Our body.*

You would have died without the operation, they argued. Failed zygotic separation, parasitic metabolism. But perched on my skull, the heaviness of her was solace, a burrow fitted perfectly to loneliness. *Your body,* she hums now into the veins where they untied her. *Our soul.* There is an intricate translation in her refusal. The way she stands in a field across from the house where we once lived. *One lamb is missing,* she mutters to the long scar above my ear, her bodiless fingers like wind around a vernal pool touching that line of her darker hair in mine.

GHOST

Today our soul began fingering the unlocked bones of my fontanelle as if trying to remember something about flesh and the strange forms that ripen there. When our soul thinks, I see between invisibles, down to where seepage has extraordinary chambers. When our soul feels, I remember how our mother set my conjoined twin before a mirror and asked, *Who is that pretty girl?* and my poor sister laid her head down on the rug, weeping. Our soul says it's hardest for my twin, living half in the fire. That's why, when my sister sleeps, our soul needs to visit her dream, and so he sets up my dark just the way I like it, and disappears. It's lonely then, but I try to remember the story of our soul's ascent: *Once upon a time, two doctors and two nurses huddled around us, cutting one head from another, but a soul is the property of infinity, and so I flew above the operating room into the blue neither.* Always our soul leaves out the part where he trembles at my bodiless head, bleeding and set aside, and then frantically turns his gaze back and forth between my twin and me. *That's okay,* I tell the lingering that our soul leaves. *No one can ever make you choose.*

SOUL

I left a light on for you, the living twin told me last time I appeared, but her eyes were glassy, elegiac. Poor thing. Each time her mother drags her to a doctor and they entomb her in the MRI, or knock lightly at her knees with a rubber hammer, I am stunned. Tell me, is there a medicine for dying in a surgical dream and waking up dead? And what about beginning with the graft of a driftless ghost? Fact is, a body can be in two places at once, but not a soul. The soul is a point man patrolling countless windows; he sees beyond the chaotic report, the strict and criminal hours, into a ponderous whole. So I can only stand before darkness coming in through two hearts, knowing that is where I should be standing: there and there. Forgive me, but lately I pretend to one that I am visiting the other, and instead fly out to a lost town up the delta. There I move among the late-night fishermen listening to their transistor radios.

In One of Ten Thousand Versions

I have a penis and I use it wisely,
holding it out for the swallows

who need to pause between empires
they are building under the bridge,

or as the clumsy brush of a kindergartner
painting the trees

under an extraordinary confusion of stars.
In summer, my penis doubles as ballast and keel

for my kayak bumping down the American river,
egrets lifting off with prehistoric groans.

And speaking of history, I don't insult my penis
by confusing it with an armored tank

leveling a foreign slum. I don't holster
or pack heat, don't whip mongrels

with barbed wire. No my penis is not a larva
feeding on victory, swelling into a packed grenade,

hoarse from shouting at the opposing halfback.
My penis is simply a voice box for desire,

not exactly deaf, but limited in its knowledge
of sign language. It can gesture *More. I want more.*

It can point like the Rabbi's long-handled yad
at women made shapely with time—

their gaze shattered by adolescence,
then pieced back together with burden—

because my penis knows loveliness
must be anointed, must be touched

as if it were parchment inscribed
with the delicate shadow of God. Believe me,

there is a science to loving the penis,
and I have studied its vulnerability

before the presence of mystery,
as it quivers like a dowsing stick

before the river of my wanting
and leaps to announce

that I need to be held in the igneous face
of longing, at least that part of me

still willing to catch fire, to burn.

In Another Version, I Have a Child with God

A girl this time. He coos and chortles with a joy
that shouldn't surprise me, having seen Daffodil Hill
and quince orchards blossom in spring.

Still it's sweet, how the big guy kneels beside her crib,
and then pops up like a newly exploded solar system,
crowing, *Peek-a-boo, now you see Me, now you don't!*

Which is how I feel about the night feedings
He promised to share. In fact, with few exceptions,
He's not much different from my first husband—

His critically important errands
just when the baby's diapers need changing.
Or how I ask Him for tomatoes and a pint of half-and-half

and He comes back with a bushel of horned melon
and three goats rescued from a cliff in Crete. *Honey,* I say,
you are hopeless, and He smiles like a meteor shower,

which sets the baby laughing
at all the electromagnetic neutrinos dazzling the walls,
which only amplifies His pleasure,

until sometimes I have to insist He stop
before we all spontaneously combust.
Which He says is impossible, *Darling, be rational.*

This is where we get into our arguments
about reason and mystery, what with His claims
to have created a universe in a week

when He can't even fold the laundry before bed.
But despite all the critiques on His cruelty and arrogance,
or the outright lies about His homophobia

and pro-life agendas, you have no idea
how often He cries at night when He thinks I'm asleep,
poring over His species,

weeping for the laughing owl, Cuban holly,
or Xerces, the last blue butterfly.
Just reading the *Times,* He can take a millennium

over the lists of Iraqi dead, touching each name
as if fingering an original spark blundered into darkness.
On Sundays, He stares out the window

at our unmowed lawn, devising good dreams
for the terminally ill. Other times, He watches the baby sleep,
her flawless lips parted in a plump collision,

and shakes His head, whispering, *Honey, what was I thinking?*
How could I have gotten it so right
and wrong at the same time?

This is when I gather His immensity into my arms
and croon, *Shhhhh. What about the pomegranates*
with their cathedrals of scarlet? What about the taste of it

and the fire of the actual flaring in a single afternoon
among the aspens? What about a body
meaning everything it cannot say

while all night, wave by wave,
the wild, uncoded sea
quietly unloads its portage of yesterday's winds?

In a Later Version

The Russians and Cubans play soccer in a corn maze.
It's hard to tell who runs around lost in the rustling,
and who scores a goal, but it is clear there is only one side,

so it doesn't matter who wins, it's simply another excuse for happiness
with a great deal of cheering and back-slapping. Best of all,
sitting on a lawn chair among a small crowd of spectators,

I'm still young and pretty. You can tell it in the gaze of men
as I adjust my sundress, though soon it will become
abundantly clear that the allure belongs to my daughter,

at sixteen, and this is her dream stolen from the tweed couch
where she naps, cheeks flushed, lips parted red as cardinals,
her textbooks fallen to the floor, astir in a breeze. And okay,

I am a woman in my fifties, washing dishes
before a window with its dispatches of sky and sunlight,
listening to the faint clank of a schooner

anchored in our cove, its sails battered and beaten into rags,
the neighbor's son buried on the hills across this bay,
and this his astonished boat

no one can bear to ask his mother to drag back in.
Because everyone knows a parent is mostly animal
and fierce in her accumulation of the beautiful

as it blows apart. And anyone can see how the pages
from my daughter's history text turn
to one color-plated catastrophe after another—

the sea outside this window necklaced with wind,
its pleats like furrows where the dead could plant a field.
There, between vanishings, it would be enough for them.

In Another Version, I Play Gin Rummy with Satan

Who is surprisingly lame at cheating. *Hey*, I protest,
as I see him slip apart the cards, though his gaze reminds me

that calling out the King of Hell is a tad ironic. That
and the pelican washed up at water's edge, its wingspan

stitched and overlaid in brown and white,
as if it was nothing to lay ravage and beauty so close together.

Satan gulps his beer, teeters backward in his chair,
belches like a third-world sewage system.

I keep expecting wind to bring a bad scent of pelican,
but that poor bird is freshly downed, untouched for now

by vultures or maggots, only a couple of blood-red holes
gouged into its body. Holes like gunshots. Like a crime.

This is protected land, a national treasure—Satan laughs,
looking up over his cards, red eyes gleaming, *Really?*

You want to call in the ranger? You? With your unleashed dog?
Your expired fishing license?

His eternal belly butts up against the table's edge
like July in the Central Valley with its ripe orbs glowing

under a demonic sun. Still, his acrimony is reassuring,
because anger means a bad hand and sure enough,

Satan mutters *Shit!* and slaps an ace onto the discard pile.
Which would be great except that suddenly I realize

we never agreed on what's at stake: world peace,
a second mortgage, one of my kids? Satan swigs his brew

and stares at me impatiently. If only we had shaken hands
before playing, agreed it's just a game, no one gets hurt.

If only I knew what I needed and what would prove burden.
Jesus! Satan says. *Just play.* If only I could gnaw on

another archetype. *Take your goddamn turn,* Satan barks, and then,
impossibly, improbably, the draw pile flashes so fast

I'm not sure I saw it flutter, but it does, and I know already
my three of hearts waits there like the little atom of love

that drew it forth, and I am grinning, flush with my micro-orgasm
of victory—until I raise my gaze up to the empty chair.

Oh that miserable son of a bitch, tickled pink by his punkish thievery,
even as he races off to the next sucker—

and it may be the raven barking from the cypress grove,
or a motorcycle growling on the highway across this bay—

but I swear I can hear the Prince of Darkness snicker
as he watches his next victim arrange her draw

of genetic blessings or tax-deductible donations,
that she imagines, just this once, could trump the Devil's hand.

All Night You Ask the Children of the World to Forgive You

For polar melt, acid rain, the last blue whale.
For big box stores laid on top of bobcats,
wild iris, vernal pools, trackless skies.
And of course, for greed and envy,
rape and horror, the neighbor's Hummer
parked over another angel of experience
busy sewing feathers
onto the thousands dead, the child soldiers,
a young woman strapping her body to a bomb.
And if not all night, at least once a week,
you ask for worldlight, sunlight,
the abundant longshot,
tease of unending delight,
slant fate of riches for them, for theirs,
for all the children, but especially
for this girl, your youngest
calling you out at dusk.
On the cooling walk,
she crouches beside a black stray.
He purrs like a factory of pleasure.
Arches up to meet her palm.
She wants to know if it's just in movies
that cats drink milk.
And then, out of nowhere, asks,
Mom, I forget, what was nine eleven?
Do you answer?
Or rub behind the creature's ears,
down his thin back.
Look out at the street oaks
moving lazily in wind
and say, *I don't remember.*

Then all night ask the children of the world
to forgive you for cowardice,
passivity, the simple lie.

III

magnitude

At the Zoo

Pausing before a panther pacing savagely,

black testicles swinging,
heart smoldering in its half-lit house,

I ask my father if he believes in God.

A flock of peacocks has gathered near his wheelchair.
They chase each other, shrieking.

Silently my father watches them run in circles,

then answers, *No.*
I'm fairly certain that this is all there is,

and smiles at me, not ungladly.

Even the eucalyptus are ponderous with song.
In the world just before his going,

I could watch him
watch those wingless birds a long time.

Their spectral iridescence,
their small revolutions of shine.

The Viewing

Angular, your cheek colder than the room,
you must have slept on ice all night,
a white blanket tucked underneath your arms.
And under that, your unknown nakedness
laid out like a shadow loose in wind.
Behind us someone has carefully arranged
two chairs, a table with an unlit candle.
I touch your calves,
the shocking softness of your feet.
Let my hand linger on your forehead,
then pull a few silver hairs
and lay them in a Kleenex,
before awkwardly dropping my head
onto your chest. Nothing
but an untouchable history
between us. Everything after
asleep on your lips.

The First Spring Since You Died

begins, of course, with rain tamping down the soil.
Rain arguing with what is dormant, what is not—
a raccoon pawing through trash,
the groaning rumble of a train.
And it's there that I can feel you
trying to remember your body—
the word *hello,* or *yes,* rolled inside your mouth,
your heart throwing its pulse
like a red ball against your chest,
until I whisper, *It's okay Dad, go back to sleep.*
And then it's lighter, the rain stops and starts.
Daffodils inch nearer to explosion.
By morning, the homeless men
outside my office roll up their blankets.
Take up their corner posts.
I give money to the first that asks
so that I never have to choose.
Like the day you told me, *Don't come, I'll be fine,*
so I unpacked my clothes, put up my suitcase,
and then you died.
Now the fruiting plums
bud young and pink.
The sky festers with jays and crows.
Listening, you might think that spring
was just another assault on eternity,
what with all those snowbells
stringing pearly mines,
a blood-hot seething of the tulips.
Tomorrow wiring the fields
to a wet and searing gold.

Now and Then

He is never dead when I ask him
how many stations between grief and rapture.

And I don't know what he can hear
over this sea cursing in a gale wind,

though certainly it's not mercy
or even comfort that I expect.

It's simply what goes on ahead
shadowing the steep cauldron of this bay.

I tell myself to breathe.
Pull my lifejacket tighter.

Our last night with him, it hurt my own chest to listen.
He gasped and spoke and gasped again.

Outside his window, a bird with a yellow blaze
waited and sang. His last night with us,

I kissed my father on the mouth.
The bird had already gone, though I never saw it go.

Today the water wrestles with a slow anger,
a blistered slate of spark and rain.

I wish my father had told me
how death remembers the living

as a story that being tells itself.
A story about loneliness

broken into now and then.

I Tell My Dead Father a Secret

If you remember California

in October, leaf litter and pollen
spun into a destroying radiance.

If you remember radiance,

how the year's last spit of heat
makes a glass coffin of our windows.

There, on the counter, a frame from our hive
sweats honey into a baking pan.

If we had lifted the frames more slowly,
had not slid them in so quickly,

there would still be brood in the chambers,
a queen to spark the soft center of time.

If you remember time

and its honey like an exploding box of light.

If you remember light.

The days are so short now, we wake in the dark.
The workers are tireless.

Even at night, ear pressed to the hive,
we can hear their thrum,

a million tiny wings warming the queen
their bodies tell them is still there.

If you remember a body.

Sometimes when I can't sleep
I come down to the kitchen

and cut a bit of comb from the frame,
until I can taste darkness

broken into its undeniable sheen.

If you remember stars,

before you woke cold and crushed inside an urn,
dusk undressing the fragrant spell of oak.

That last afternoon in your wheelchair,
you confessed,

"When you were a child,
I was wrong to hurt you."

Do you remember cruelty?

Our carelessness doomed the body of the bees.

Without a body, is there shame?

In spring, we will sweep the glowing engine
of another swarm into a box, and start again.

Do you remember beginning?

This afternoon, braiding my daughter's hair
on a bench before the sea,

it seemed I was binding
last summer's light and wind together.

If you remember wind.

How it cannot be held even as it touches.
How I pretended my fingers were yours,

and those sunlit strands in her hair,
mine, all mine.

Instruments of Loss and Wind

The last time the bay lay half in glitter and half in fog,
he was dying, and so I waited, alert to the world

that had made him, and, so I reasoned,
knew best how he should be dissembled.

So too, this morning, low clouds snag on cliffs,
a grey pelt blown open to sun,

while the sparse pines remain black on the distant shore.
Perhaps this strange halving and doubling of light

is how the sky quarrels with the sound caught inside my dream
of swimming as I once did, laid against his back,

his arms pulling us through the dark pastures of the bay.
Perhaps the argument is orchestral,

a score the wind plays on the shadow's instrument—
one more variation on the many about love

and how close we must come, at the end,
without looking away. Because this morning,

there is another whiteness edging nearer, floating closer,
finally stepping on shore, a black gaze fixed on mine,

until eventually I give this gull my father's name,
and it is like happiness or breath, god, for once

having nothing to say, before he rises and is gone.

Letter to My Newly Widowed Mother

All day a seal rose and disappeared into the bay,
as if looking back at an old familiar body
he'd left behind. A vulture unsettles the cypress.
Soon the winged ants will rise up from the floorboards
and chrysalis will float through ancient stands of oaks.
At this hour, I wish you could hear the deer
as they travel down the ridge, snap brush.
In the morning, the beach will be scattered
with shells and hoof prints
where they paused
and touched their lips to shore.
Sometimes when I think of you alone
in my father's study, staring out the window,
I like to imagine your loneliness as a doe
nibbling on the willows, brushing up against a pine,
easy in her body, its wild solitude.

IV

risking delight

Poem Ending with an Unanswered Question

As if two girls could wear that green
like a dress of portent or memory—

whole fields of it laid down by rain—

they run through the pasture
shouting, arms spread out,
    chasing the farmer's Holsteins into thunder.

In the distance, someone's father hammers at the gate.
    Yells something at the girls,

and they stop, sit down.

Then stretch across the wet grass,
arms braided over their heads,
    and roll down the slope,
            hurtling one into another.

Soon enough lust and time will blister
the flat boards of their bodies.

Tell me,
        why is there is no angel
mortal enough to keep even one childhood
                everlasting?

Last night, they slept together on a narrow bed,
their faces so perfectly undressed of wariness—
                it hurt

to look, to wonder
        which is crueler, memory or forgetting?

Adultery

It was impossible to cleave him from me.

There were signs of another woman
in our daughter's neatly braided hair

and how, in dreams, I kept hearing him

like a radio playing music from a car
driven into sea.

I wish I had known then the whole story of myself.
How an isolated fact is as close to a lie as any other.

Mostly I hate the hinge I called into being

that late afternoon on the porch, our daughter not yet three.
I remember looking out at hail, its gorgeous shatter,

the way the blue was bitten with icy petals.

Back then, her hair was so blonde,
if you combed it with your fingers,

the lifted strands fell like blown snow.

She was weeping.
Asking why her father would not come home.

I was trying to find the smallest, simplest words I could,

forgetting how innocence works:
the first time you name betrayal,

it exists.

you tell me the end

has happened already
                        is traveling toward us   the double star of Sirius
                                                exploding into a black hole
                        our universe swallowed into itself
                with such force everything becomes essential
                                                        atomic   elemental
                        the earth erased into vapor

and if there is a part of the soul that fights death
                that doesn't believe in losing even a single afternoon
                                        waves frayed and split   the wind
                        banging against an osprey   our girls at dusk
                turning cartwheels across the reddened sand
                                                        then why
                        does grief feel so at home inside us

our wonder a kind of singing
                that comes from far beyond the self
                                        the way touch renders us speechless
                        your hands on my back   our mouths salty and alive
                while behind us water keeps on pouring into the bay's
                                                        enormous room
                                that cannot hold us   that never promised to
hold us here for long

Inheritance

What parents leave you
is their lives.
—FRANK BIDART, "Lament for the Makers"

All afternoon, our daughters in sundresses take turns
posing barefoot before the camera, blonde hair flying.

We sit beside the shore watching the stubborn gold
of their limbs twist and leap,

the live oak and blue gum
letting go into lush spans of heat. Now there is nothing

they have not taken from our hunger.
At dusk, the hours pack up their light,

while we shake out towels, rinse plates in the sea.
The stars wait for everyone to go home.

Say that love is a darkroom ripening their brightness.
Say that rapture travels like a bird

through the open windows of our plunder,
singing all the while to make the silence wild.

In the Real Paradise

There are seven strings of birdsong,

a brief percussive flash
as a Steller jay and nuthatch brawl inside a pine.

And of course, there is our youngest,

the child we almost didn't have,
throwing driftwood off the dock.

There is a hatch of flies to swoon and plummet
in the seaweed, the musseled crust of shore.

There is everything we desire,

but still don't have.

Like the farmer's cows our daughter has wanted
more than half her life to touch.

Or, in the hour of her deepest sleep,
you and I, unclothed. After all these years,

still unsure. Still a little shy.

Menarche

The moon in August is the color of sand,
and shines on this child stroking the hen gone broody.

That first summer I bathed her in this sink
and sometimes, in the kitchen window,

her untried lips would part and close,
as if she were swallowing light.

It was a completeness that haunted me.
Blossoms on the peach and pluot trees.

In my hands, her entire weight.
A completeness, now torn by time.

I remember the weeks she spent
teaching the chickens to fly.

How she'd toss one up above the perch,
and then command, *Down!*

her hands netted underneath
to catch their bodies. Tonight

I watch her kneel in their coop.
An owl warns softly across the fields.

I know she is unwilling.
But the body is an animal too

that must sleep and wake,
while small winds thread down the delta.

Does she feel it yet—how the slightest breeze
unlocks the last few doors of dark,

opens the entire house of sky?

When the Door Between Worlds Finally Opened

I found myself at the sink where she lay asleep
in a bath, light ripening the window.

And if the moment was about the unknown
perfecting itself in form—

a faint snow of down swirled across her skull,
ten fingers capped in ten tiny pearls—

it was a revelation and a betrayal, too,
this whole before consciousness,

this evanescence resetting the world
one loss at a time.

It was apprehension before I could name it,
and then it was after,

and already she was thirteen,
carrying buckets of feed stall to stall,

calling out to the roan, the bay,
in a voice strangely like my own.

Before separation and its invention of longing,
there was the silence where she once woke

patiently staring up at me
as if I was a place the sky should have been.

And of that drowse and lush permission
almost nothing remains.

Only my banishment.
Only a glimpse, now and then,

out my car window
of a girl cantering along the farmer's slough.

The Raccoon

Dusk wakes the den beneath the house.

A female climbs from the congregational warmth,
her ringed tail sweeping the deck.

At the glass doors, she stares in,
lifts onto her haunches.

Around us, our clothes are scattered
like ephemera, like the moment
turning physical before it vanishes.

On the table, our meal untouched.
Wineglasses glint through a spill of light.

Behind her, we can hear the sea
rework the silence.

It's not exactly starting over,

but whatever breaks the body
into handfuls of flesh and time, flaw and blessing,

has summoned its hopeful shadow
near the joining, has left us watching
her dark hands at the door.

We Sit in a Beached Rowboat

beside each other, facing out to sea.
Just beyond us, the dock has broken free
so that the rotted planks of the ramp
fall now, unworshipped, into deep water.
How deftly one version has vanished—
our daughters standing there in nightgowns and boots,
their flashlights trained on a wild boil of shiners,
or lying on the sun-warmed deck,
shirts pulled up,
setting a handful of newts free
across each other's skin.
Already those children are too far away,
too small to rescue, and it is growing dark.
In the cliffs above us, the deer rise up
from their crushed beds of grass.
Around them, rings of blue gilia
shut their delicate purses of seed.
Soon Venus and the North Star
will enter the sky's deepening meadow.
Already this is the version
where time is made beautiful
with waiting.
Where everything breakable in you
appears to me so often,
so easily now—

Leave-Taking

How suddenly good-bye occupies the deepest place in us.
So the shy ghosts of deer stop and stare

at chrysalis and leaf jitter shifting in the vast fires of wind.
All being is processional. It makes a sound like a scar,

the path poorly translated into corridors of willow.
Already our truck, loaded with mattresses and cookpans,

grinds one last time over the cattle guards onto the highway.
Behind us, darkness plumps the emptiness.

Touches with all its plant and animal hands
through a diaspora of doors. If only we could stay,

listening to claws clicking on the linoleum, an army
of mandibles dissembling the weathered timbers,

we'd see the outside has waited so long to enter
that now it arrives like prophecy, a wild fecundity

taking up where it left off—
wood-rats weaving strands of our hair into nests,

bats chiming through shattered windows,
comet scars ripening in a roofless bowl of sky.

Eventually

There will be a reckoning with joy and its aftershock:
        a family poised together under the burn of pistache,
                finches gathered on the lawn like a latch in sunlight.

And though there will be no tragedy beyond the usual unfastening,
        it will begin with wind turning the pages of dominion,
            and children, dressed as soldiers,

marching lantern-like into a gone summer. Afterwards,
        a heron will groan as it unfolds over the bay,
                water glistening like skin beneath an opened blouse,

one daughter dragging a suitcase to her car, the other
        cantering a quarterhorse through the farmer's fields.
            Nothing exotic or unbound,

no unseemly disclosures or armies rising up
        like crop circles around them—no, it will be an ordinary
            banishment, rich with surrender,

desire splitting the joinery into time.
        And yet, for a while under the trembling pistache,
            a man and woman will hold hands, dazed

and small, wondering how abundance vanishes so quickly
        into a sky carved with birds, a winged and yellow chaos
            exploding into air, drifting slowly down.

V

music despite everything

Tahoe Wetlands

Here the ground sings,
      the marshes whir with invisible coots and swans.
                      Here the self is a flyway
           over the hieroglyphics of wheel and track,
      and the winged husk that was my hovering
just beyond his body's piston.

Each summer these rice fields burn to carbon.
      Each winter, rain pours into the rutted cradles
                    the way the nurse
         passed her hands across the bruise
      his gun forced into my thigh.
Time is like this kind of light,

equal parts ravage and mercy
      striking the berm black, the brush gold,
                 the molten edges
        lifting a flock of tundra swans
      into the Sierra's remote shoulders.
Finally, the years have drained his shadow

into the pond's mirror-finish. Now all that remains
      is what vengeance spawned:
                 a wish like bones
        scattered after the kill,
      a voice pulled from ice, wind rattling the cattails.
If you could have seen me that morning—

new mother, new wife,
      crawling this half mile over mud
                 into my soon-to-be

ex-husband's arms, you might ask,
        Is the violence over? No,
first the self must join prayers

with its collapse. No, it takes a long time
        to learn how to lose everything.

Tahoe City, 1988

I want to tell it again as the story of two lovers
meeting in a park just before winter,
a light frost crusting the fields.

I want him to appear small and forsaken
beneath the immense vault of the Sierras,
his hood pulled away from his face.

A kingdom of starlings
lifts from the nearly bare branches,
one wave of disturbance becoming another,

as he watches me run, his hands in his pockets,
and I want him frozen between doubt
and a blaze of desire.

As for those birds setting back down,
I want the last few leaves they've knocked into air
to fall as apology, an error in tense.

And even if I can't decide
whether sun kindles the lawn,
or the first snow is waiting just under the hour,

every story must happen in time. In time
his gun slips from its sheath,
presses cold to my temple.

Here, no language for asking,
no jacket to lay between dirt and my face.
And because truth is a current

that both enters and carries the story,
here the story wrestles with silence,
and here it returns as a ghost,

as he shoves his gun back in his pocket,
bends to my ear, wet lips muttering,
"That's all I wanted,"

his boots kicking up a clatter of birdsong,
a feather sifting violet over the trail.

Ode to Fruit Flies

They lend a sparse fur to the air
just above the bananas,

or hover like a small cloud
over the cut daffodils on my table,

while two or three
tread wings in a glass of wine.

Urge and urge and urge, Whitman wrote
about the coming apart,

the coming differently back again.
When I woke this morning

there were yellow tulips opening in the garden.
I stood at the sink, filling the kettle,

and looked out at each corseted flower.
In my dream, wind was tossing a child

between trees, and my father had returned
from death

to catch her just in time. Sometimes
I need the truth close and in my face.

Sometimes when I no longer wish
to be diminished, the very air flares—

sudden hallelujahs
strung like jostled, tiny lanterns

across the changing mind of sky.

Songbird

Listen—

nothing is more damned than joy.
Like the fine pain of a papercut
on the lips of a desperate plea,

let it enter—

the unheard falling of a colossal pine
and its armature, its delicate green ceilings
adrift on a cloud of earth.

If the idea of delay is prayer,

if the sky suffers in its weightless swinging
between branches, perhaps song itself
is a prelude to brokenness—

velvet indentation

of something thrown down,
a vireo floating face up in grass
like a small excerpt of silence,

a golden visible

lashed to a darker wing.
Listen—even if narcissus burn
in acrid welters of yolk and petal,

even if the orchard

        explodes in downy shrapnel,
    still, the world was made from divided parts
and passed through

                    on its way to a larger shining.

Yes to the Youth at an Outdoor Concert

Because today they are everywhere, supple
and flushed with something just lit.
Even the cows raise their heads from the fields to stare.
The boys are shirtless, their backs sinewy and marbled.
And the girls in sundresses, all slope and cleavage
like these mounded hills fired up
in the extravagance of mustard, new grass.
Sure, they will drink too much, redden and burn.
In the car behind me, there is the flare
of a lighter, a pipe passed around.
But this is the hour of the zenith.
This is the first afternoon of real heat
when the forget-me-nots and columbine and bush lupine
clamor and swell, the mule ears flare,
when new buds turn inside out the earth's hunger,
fragile arches of the petals
offering up a thousand little doors.
And why not enter wherever you can?
Why not let them dive together
into another round of joy and longing,
before they learn the names for brevity?
Why not gather up a kingdom of the newly risen
and rub their bodies together into fire?

Garden Party as the Prow of a Small Ship Traveling

Above the blue-glass goblets,
        mismatched plates, something winged but crying persists.
Presses in on a June evening,
        the tornado warning finally lifted, the ribeye cooked
to rare perfection. Kumquats burn
        inside the tree's low cage like a brilliance troubled into fire.
Someone has marinated oranges
        in wine. Wrapped trout in bacon. Someone says,
They are probably owlets
        in a nestbox, frightened and hungry, so that now the cries
separate into three, you think,
        one a little higher, one more rhythmic against the third
screeching for the parent wings,
        the fresh kill. On the roof, a hivebox hums.
Someone built those bees
        a cupboard, those owls a box, as if to make a sanctuary
deep inside creation
        as it unravels, layer upon accelerating layer.
Someone asks you to pass
        your plate. Now take a different vantage,
say from infinity's lookout.
        There, destruction has its opportunities for variance. Look
at those Icelandic poppies,
        their fanfare and ruddy cups ruthlessly throwing themselves
open, the star-threads of columbine
        sipping at the unforeseen. Look at the sensual doors
of the mouths beside you,
        opening and closing around the edges of pleasure,
a hoisted cake lit by candles,
        voices gathered into an arsenal of the colloquial,
the well-intentioned. Yes,
        everyone is born inside time's appetite for more.

Live, live, live, you hear
        in the homesick hour of the clock, *hurry, hurry, hurry,*
in the warning minutes
        of the hatchlings, their audible derangement vexing
the night's thickening stars.

Variations on Rupture and Repair: Horse

It was summer, whatever that was—
slow landscape of heat and sprinklers,
the last cherries falling in a bloody circle
around the tree, the sound of a firing range
just beyond the pines.
My daughter had asked me to turn out
the coal black horse—
his enormous hooves like iron hammers,
his sweat-damp flanks like cannons
locked against my shoulders.
And my heart, that clock of many inside one,
banging away
as if to build itself another shelter,
a better one with fewer doors.
I stepped inside his stall and took the rope,
calling out his name.
Swallows rustled in the rafters, dust spiraling after.
He laid his muzzle across my shoulder
the way a fine wind touches sand,
the heat and scent of the world in him.
And he neither led nor followed,
but plodded so close beside me
his darkness kept knocking mine,
as if carrying something of the unbearable
between us until it could be borne.

Interlude

In September, the wind surprisingly warm

after such a cool summer, we stand in the farmer's fields
and pick the last blackberries to make it into ripeness.

Shaft and aftershaft of clouds wheel across the pasture.
Vultures circle like winged erasers.

Angry marks crosshatch your arms, but you refuse a jacket,

meaning, you want to feel the thorns, the irrevocable flowering.
The part of time no one can touch.

Deeper in, I find a hollowed-out copse of cattails
where the blacktail sleep, a few seeds of milkweed drifting down.

What if there is no death, only moments looking elsewhere?

What if this is what listening does—
the hour dissembled down to its smallest eternity,

the still light of dusk slipping like water over Black Mountain?

As for my can of berries, poorly ripened, but brimming,
they have traveled a particular weather

to reach this chirring, all the small particles of sound
changing into evening,

a few bats flying out like black kites between the trees.

And you, who have had your share of sorrow,
the kind that complicates the body, dirties the spirit,

call back in answer
from deep inside this lush and sharpened thicket,

Yes, I have more than enough,

and mean it.

Variations on Rupture and Repair: Cottage

Hidden inside ceanothus
and a bed of wild poppies,
it was unlocked
when we knocked, entered in.
I want to say we touched nothing.
That the silence inside that strange room
did not say, *Lie down, undress,*
while our vigilance sorted out the tonalities
of a crow outside the window
from the orchestral hush of the sea down below.
I want to say that we were altered
by our hidden inventories of longing,
when, simply, there was an unfamiliar bed
covered in a blue comforter, three down pillows,
and a damp stain when we rose up.
We knew it was trespass,
and yet there was a tenderness in your hands
at the washbasin, a little slip of soap
pressed against the coverlet, wetted and foaming,
like a spirit going over and over the world
of what it already knows.
Perhaps there are blessings
that blossom outward from violation.
Perhaps we had to enter through a new door
to rise differently, glad to have fallen
from the wings we meant to put back on,
from the myths we needed to walk through
into the incandescence of our ordinary lives.

In Praise of What Remains

After he left you on the wrong side of beautiful,

your body thrown like a coat onto the ground,
your mouth scraped clean of mud, his gun still cold.

Afterwards in the snowblue light of November,
there was a list, numbered, but not yet filled in.

The nurse apologized before asking you to undress,
her hands smelling of someone else's hurt and soap.

The list went on like anything wanting to be healed:

all that green-gold light after rain,
compressed sweetness in a little rip of time,

your daughter gluing a tiny fence around her model
of the Santa Inez mission, truth backlit by harm.

Still there was an argument you could not enter

without sitting inside the miniature chapel
on benches made from toothpicks, windows wrapped in plastic.

On one side it was winter, wind raking a frozen river,
and you, sealed into an elegant nullity.

On the other, you stood riverside, gasping
at two humpback whales circling the Port of Sacramento,

the delicate anchor of a new child
asleep in your arms,

those barnacled, blade-scarred bodies
breaching like the paired lungs of God.

And by argument, you mean the atonal, the dissonant,
the ways you break to this inelegance and need,

the boy in your office, face down in the carpet,
screaming, *I'm starving, help me, help me!*,

the wind outside your windows
whipped into a firmament,

a fiery snow of leaves driven down.
Surely there is something more than endurance

to believe in, something more sanctified
than a child throwing his hard skull

into your chest, something larger than one body
soothing another

until his terror slows and he laps milk from a bowl
underneath your desk. Months later

his grandmother will tell you how she found him
in a trailer, covered in his mother's blood.

Awake and mute in the dead woman's arms.
You want so much to say *God bless you*,

and know what the hell it means.
Even now, trash plowed into gutters,

you walk past a grape arbor alive with sound,
and except for a yellow flash, a wincing shadow,

the moment's aria is invisible, the choral exultation
scattershot and winged.

Finally, there are entire moments
      in which you glance at the huckleberries,
blue and salted among the leaves,
      the poppies blaring face up
like emboldened cardinals,
      and forget you are evicted,
your cottage empty as this rowboat
      chained to a single, sunken weight,
the bleached dock kneeling as it drowns.
      Say your life is a closed circle
where a dirge bobs in waves,
      cormorants batting their wings
against the forgiving chord of water.
      Say mercy,
but mean erasure takes you tenderly apart.
      This afternoon when you arrived,
a crowd of children dragged rubber boats
      in and out of the bay, laughing.
A shirtless toddler sat on sand, licking her shovel.
      Pointed to the jellyfish
that pulsed like an understory of halos.
      Soon ash will be snowing down,
vagrants burning the floorboards
      and closet doors. Say nothing,
which is the original evensong.
      Or say that repetition
and its elixir of details
      belongs to salvation,
while the next world comes to you
      inside of this one, inexplicable
and strange. August,

the bay is a sky of ghosts.
Moonjellies, one brother tells another,
and holding hands,
they wade out with pails.

NOTES

"St. Augustine, Florida"—for D.P.

"All Night You Ask the Children of the World to Forgive You"—the title is taken from a line by Robert Dana in his poem "Written in Winter."

"Garden Party as the Prow of a Small Ship Traveling"—for Djina.

"Variations on Rupture and Repair: Horse"—in gratitude to Annemarie Flynn, and to Dan Bellm's poem "The Weight."

"Interlude"—for Nancy.

CPSIA information can be obtained at www.ICGtesting.com
Printed in the USA
BVOW03s1724080114

341214BV00002B/14/P